2 7 APR 2011		
2 1 OCT 2011		
2 1 SEP 2013		

Camouflage

Copyright © QED Publishing 2004

First published in the UK in 2004 by
QED Publishing
A division of Quarto Publishing plc
The Fitzpatrick Building
188–194 York Way, London N7 9QP

A Catalogue record for this book is available from the British Library.

ISBN 1 84538 002 9

Written by Terry Jennings
Designed by Zeta Jones
Editor Hannah Ray
Picture Researcher Joanne Beardwell

Series Consultant Anne Faundez
Creative Director Louise Morley
Editorial Manager Jean Coppendale

Printed and bound in China

Picture credits

Key: t = top, b = bottom, m = middle, c = centre, l = left, r = right

Corbis/Linda Lewis 12–13, /Buddy Mays 4, /Roger Tidman 8; **Ecoscene**/Frank
Blackburn 6–7, /Satyendra Tiwari 20–21, 23br; **Getty Images**/Daryl Balfour
14, /Wayne R Bilenduke 10–11, 22tl, /John Downer 15, /Nick Garbutt 18, /Peter
Lilja 19, /Karen Su 16–17, 22bl, /Tom Walker 9; **Still Pictures**/Yves Thonnerieux
5, 23tr.

QED
START
Talking

Camouflage

Terry Jennings

QED Publishing

QED

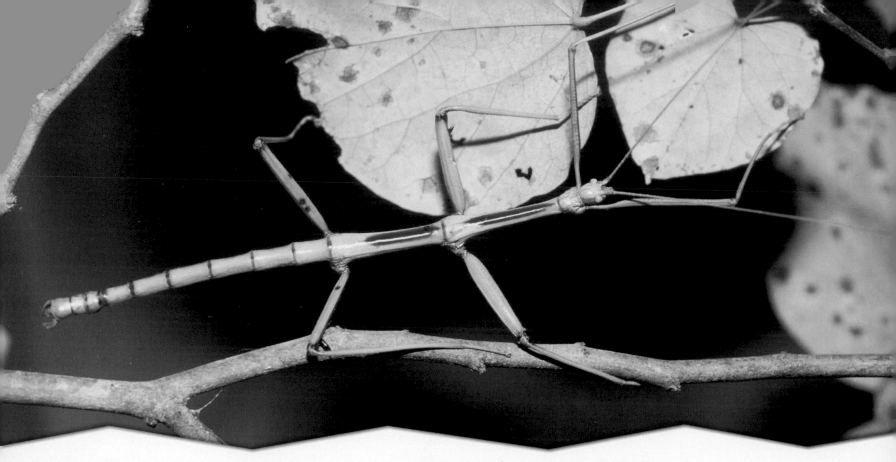

Some animals use their colour to help them to hide and keep safe.

4

This way of hiding is
called camouflage.

The male pheasant is easy to see.

Can you see the female pheasant looking for food?

7

This animal is a stoat.
In summer, it is brown.

In winter, the stoat turns white. Why does it do that?

The polar bear lives in a place where it is always snowy.

The polar bear's white fur makes it hard to see her and her cubs against the snow.

The plaice has a
flat body.

Can you see
this fish when it
is on the bottom
of the sea?

13

Can you see the lioness
in the long grass?

This lioness is hunting. Why does she have to run fast?

The tiger has stripes on its body.

The stripes help to hide the tiger in the long grass when it is hunting.

The chameleon can
change colour quickly.

This means that it is
always camouflaged.

The deer's brown colour makes it hard to see against the leaves.

Can you remember which other animal is the same colour as the snow?

Why does the tiger have stripes?

Can you spot the camouflaged butterfly? What does it look like?

Here is another animal hiding in the leaves. Can you remember what it is called?

Carers' and teachers' notes

- Young children will need help pronouncing words such as 'chameleon' and 'pheasant', but once they have mastered these words, they enjoy repeating them. It may be necessary to explain the male and female pheasant in terms of 'Daddy' and 'Mummy'.

- Look at pages 4 and 5 together. Can your child spot the camouflaged animals? (Stick insect and butterfly.)

- Look through the rest of the book. Does your child know the names of any of the animals? What colour are the animals?

- What colour are the animals that live in the snow? What colour is the snow?

- Turn to pages 22 and 23. Look at each of the photographs and, together, talk about possible answers to the questions.

- Cut out paper butterflies in different colours and place them on a variety of coloured surfaces around your home/classroom. Which are the easiest to see? Which are camouflaged?

- Paint some clean lollipop sticks green and others brown. Scatter some of the sticks on a lawn and some on bare soil. Which are easier to see?

- Observe birds in a garden or a park. Which of them have camouflage colours?

- Carefully turn over logs or large stones. Look for small animals that are camouflaged. Be sure to replace the logs or stones exactly as they were.

- Explore movement and ask your child to move like a polar bear, a fish and a lion.

- Discuss why people such as bird-watchers need to wear clothes that camouflage them.

- Discuss why we shouldn't wear clothes that are camouflaged when we are crossing the road or walking along busy streets at night.